NORTHWEST
Coastal Wildflowers

Dana Visalli◆Derrick Ditchburn◆Walt Lockwood

hancock
house

ISBN 0-88839-518-3
Copyright © 2005 Hancock House Publishers

Cataloging in Publication Data
Visalli, Dana, 1948–
  Northwest coastal wildflowers / Dana Visalli, Derrick Ditchburn,
Walt Lockwood.

(Northwest wildflower series)
Includes index.
ISBN 0-88839-518-3

  1. Wild flowers—Northwest, Pacific—Identification. 2. Coastal
plants—Northwest, Pacific—Identification. I. Ditchburn, Derrick, 1934–
II. Lockwood, Walt, 1938- III. Title. IV. Series.

QK144.V58 2005   582'.13'0979509146   C2004-901818-3

Printed in South Korea — PACOM

Editor: Dana Visalli
Photography: Dana Visalli, Walt Lockwood, Derrick Ditchburn,
            David Hancock, Don McPhee & Mildred McPhee
Production: Rick Groenheyde, Laura Michaels, Theodora Kobald

Published simultaneously in Canada and the United States by

HANCOCK HOUSE PUBLISHERS LTD.
19313 Zero Avenue, Surrey, B.C. Canada V3S 9R9
(604) 538-1114 Fax (604) 538-2262

HANCOCK HOUSE PUBLISHERS
1431 Harrison Avenue, Blaine, WA U.S.A 98230-5005
(604) 538-1114 Fax (604) 538-2262

Website: www.hancockhouse.com
Email: sales@hancockhouse.com

Contents

INTRODUCTION

Welcome to the enchanting world of Coastal Wildflowers. The plentiful rain along the coast in the Pacific Northwest not only makes the grass greener and the trees taller than elsewhere, it also makes the flowers brighter and at times more abundant than in other areas. This little book will not only help you identify the most common flowering plants along the coast in Oregon, Washington and British Columbia, but it will draw your eye again and again to nature's colorful canvas.

Sometimes there are many look-alike species within a particular closely related group of plants. Two examples in this book are the lupines and the milkvetches. There are at least 20 species of lupines and 80 species of milkvetches in the Pacific Northwest. We will have to be satisfied in this book just to recognize these larger groups, and realize we don't know for sure exactly what species we are enjoying at any given moment.

Technical terms are avoided in the plant descriptions wherever possible; still a few do creep in. **Compound leaves** have one main leaf divided into a number of separate leaflets. If the leaflets are all joined together at a common point, like the fingers on a hand, they are **palmately compound**. If the leaflets are arranged in twos, opposite one another along the stem, like the rays on a feather, they are **pinnately compound**.

Corolla refers to all the petals of a flower, taken together (sometimes they are fused together). **Sepals** are the bracts below the petals that covered the flower bud before it opened. In the Lily Family, the sepals are often just as colorful as the petals; the two together are then referred to as **tepals**. The flowers of the Composite Family (also known as the Aster Family) are composed of many tiny flowers all combined into a circular **composite** head. What look like the petals in this group—think of what appear to be petals on a sunflower—are actually tiny flowers in their own right, called **ray flowers**. The center of a sunflower (and of many other composites) is made up of tiny **disk flowers**, which have no rays.

That should be enough to get you started. In the noisy confusion of modern life, don't forget to stop and enjoy (and then identify!) the flowers.

RED ELDERBERRY

Sambucus racemosa

Plant: A shrub or small tree, to 6 m tall.

Flower: White to creamy, 3-6 cm wide, small but numerous, crowded together in pyramidal clusters.

Fruit: Small, round, bright red fruits in large clusters.

Leaves: Pinnately compound and opposite on the stem, divided into 5-7 leaflets, sharply toothed.

Habitat: Usually in moist clearings.

Range: B.C. to California.

FRINGED GRASS OF PARNASSUS

Parnassia fimbriata

Plant: A low, leafy perennial with 1 to several flower stems 15-30 cm tall.

Flower: 5 white petals 8-12 mm long, each with a fringe of hairs at the base.

Leaves: Primarily basal, kidney-shaped leaves on long stems, with one small leaf on flower stem.

Habitat: Stream banks, wet meadows and bogs at mid- to subalpine, down to sea level in Alaska.

Range: Alaska to California.

5

SEASIDE REIN ORCHID
Platanthera greenei

Plant: An erect perennial 20-80 cm tall.
Flower: White, sweet smelling, with a long spur to 2 cm.
Leaves: Occur in basal pairs, which wither as the plant flowers late spring to summer.
Habitat: Low elevations in grassy areas and on rocky slopes.
Range: B.C. to Washington.

MAYWEED
Anthemis cotula

Plant: Branched annual 10-60 cm tall with a disagreeable odor.
Flower: A daisy-like composite with white rays (petals) and a yellow center.
Leaves: Several times divided into fine, fern-like segments.
Habitat: Fields and waste places.
Range: A native of Europe, B.C. to Oregon.

RUBIACEAE · MADDER FAMILY

NORTHERN BEDSTRAW
Galium boreale

Plant: A creeping or sprawling perennial 20-80 cm long with whorled leaves.

Flower: Tiny white flowers have 4 petals, the resulting tiny fruits have barbed hooks.

Leaves: Narrowly elliptical leaves are 2-4.5 cm long, with 4-6 of them forming a whorl (circle) around the stem.

Habitat: Moist and dry meadows, rocky slopes and forest edges, from low to high elevations.

Range: Circumboreal, Alaska to California.

ERICACEAE · HEATHER FAMILY

LABRADOR TEA
Ledum groenlandicum

Plant: An evergreen shrub .5-1.5 m tall, with rusty-hairy twigs and a spicy odor.

Flower: Clusters of 5-50 white flowers, each about 1 cm across, at twig ends.

Leaves: Narrowly elliptic, 2-6 cm long, deep green above and leathery, red-hairy below.

Habitat: Generally on wet ground in or near bogs and swamps.

Range: Alaska to Oregon.

SQUASHBERRY, HIGHBUSH CRANBERRY
Viburnum edule

Plant: A straggling to erect shrub .5-3 m tall, often with reddish bark.

Flower: Small white flowers gathered in flat-topped clusters above 2 opposite leaves.

Leaves: Distinctly 3-lobed and serrate, 3-10 cm long and nearly as wide, opposite on stem.

Habitat: Moist forests and thickets, wetland edges.

Range: Alaska to Oregon.

STINGING NETTLE
Urtica dioica

Plant: An upright perennial 1-3 m tall, with stinging hairs.

Flower: Tiny green flowers bloom in drooping clusters in the leaf axils.

Leaves: Ovate and coarsely serrate, 7-15 cm long, opposite on the stem.

Habitat: Along streams, meadows, open forests, disturbed sites, low to subalpine.

Range: Throughout North America.

RED OSIER DOGWOOD
Cornus stolonifera

Plant: A shrub to 6 m tall, usually with distinctly red stems.

Flower: 4 small white petals, each 2-4 mm long, gathered together in flat-topped clusters at branch ends.

Leaves: Elliptical, 4-12 cm long, with prominent veins, opposite one another on the stem.

Habitat: Moist soils in streamside forests and valley bottoms.

Range: In much of North America.

PALMATE COLTSFOOT
Petasites frigidus var. palmatus

Plant: A perennial with numerous stems to 50 cm tall.

Flower: Very small white flowers are clumped together in rounded heads.

Leaves: Leaves are large, mostly basal, and deeply palmately cleft, stem leaves reduced to bracts.

Habitat: Wet forests, clearings, moist roadsides, low to midelevations.

Range: B.C. to Oregon.

9

HOOKER'S FAIRY BELLS
Disporum hookeri

Plant: A few-branched, rhizomatous perennial to 70 cm tall.

Flower: White, 6-petaled flowers 1-2 cm long, in pairs below branch tips.

Fruit: 2 yellow to red berries below branch tips.

Leaves: Ovate elliptic, 5-15 cm long, with prominent veins, alternate on the stem.

Habitat: Shady woods.

Range: B.C. to Oregon.

DWARF DOGWOOD
Cornus canadensis

Plant: Low-growing, widely spreading rhizomatous sub-shrubs (woody at the base) 5-20 cm tall.

Flower: 4 white petal-like bracts 1-2.5 cm long surround several tiny clustered green flowers.

Fruit: Cluster of bright red, fleshy berries.

Leaves: 4-7 widely elliptic leaves, each 2-8 cm long, in a whorl (circle), prominently nerved.

Habitat: Moist woods.

Range: Alaska to California.

CORNACEAE · DOGWOOD FAMILY

PACIFIC DOGWOOD, FLOWERING DOGWOOD

Cornus nuttallii

Plant: A shrub to small tree, 2-20 m tall.

Flower: 4-7 large, white, petal-like bracts 2-7 cm long surround a cluster of tiny, green flowers.

Leaves: Ovate-elliptic, 4-10 cm long, with prominent veins.

Habitat: Along streams and in open to closed forests.

Range: B.C. to California.

Note: British Columbia's provincial flower.

PRIMULACEAE · PRIMROSE FAMILY

STARFLOWER

Trientalis latifolia

Plant: An upright perennial 5-20 cm tall.

Flower: 6 spreading petals, 1 to several pink or white flowers, each on a curved stalk arising from center of plant.

Leaves: 3-8 elliptic leaves, each 1.5-5 cm long, in a whorl at top of stem.

Habitat: Open forests and forest edges.

Range: B.C. to California.

INDIAN PIPE

Monotropa uniflora

Plant: Fleshy, waxy white to pinkish plant 5-25 cm tall.

Flower: White, single, narrowly bell-shaped, nodding or curved to one side.

Habitat: In humus, shaded mature coniferous forest at lower elevations.

Range: B.C. to Oregon.

Note: Indian Pipe is a saphrophyte; it obtains its nutrition from decaying wood rather than by photosynthesis.

MENYANTHACEAE · BUCKBEAN FAMILY

DEER CABBAGE

Nephrophyllidium crista-galli

Plant: A perennial aquatic or semi-aquatic with basal leaves and an upright flower stalk 20-30 cm tall.

Flower: 5-30 white flowers, each about 1 cm across in loose clusters at top of naked stem.

Leaves: Generally kidney-shaped, wider than long, 3-12 cm in width, on long stems.

Habitat: Bogs, swamps and other wet ground.

Range: Alaska to the Olympics in Washington.

ROSACEAE　　　·　　　ROSE FAMILY

INDIAN PLUM

Oemleria cerasiformis

Plant: A shrub to small tree, 1.5-4 m tall, bark purple-brown.

Flower: 5 green-white petals 5-6 mm long, fragrant flowers appear in early spring in elongate, usually drooping clusters.

Fruit: Cherry-like fruits are blue-black and very bitter.

Leaves: Elliptic, 5-12 cm long, often several attached at same point on stems.

Habitat: Dry to moist open woods, open areas like roadsides.

Range: B.C. to California.

LILIACEAE　　　·　　　LILY FAMILY

RACEME SOLOMON'S SEAL

Smilacina racemosa

Plant: A rhizomatous perennial 30-100 cm tall, often in spreading colonies.

Flower: Many tiny (2-3 mm) white flowers crowded together in an elongate cluster at stem tip.

Leaves: Broadly elliptic, 7-20 cm long, with prominent, parallel veins.

Habitat: Moist woods and stream banks to open woods.

Range: Throughout much of North America.

OCEAN SPRAY
Holodiscus discolor

Plant: A branching, upright shrub 1-3 m tall.

Flower: Large, pyramidal clusters of tiny (5 mm across) white flowers at branch tips.

Leaves: Ovate, both lobed and serrate, 4-8 cm long, woolly-hairy below.

Habitat: Coastal bluffs and dry to moist woods.

Range: B.C. to California.

ENGLISH PLANTAIN
Plantago lanceolata

Plant: A perennial with basal leaves and a narrow, upright flower stalk 10-60 cm tall.

Flower: Greenish-white and tiny, with the corolla lobes 2 mm long, the flowers crowded into a pencil-like, upright spike.

Leaves: All basal, long and narrow, 5-20 cm long and 1.5-6 cm wide, with parallel veins.

Habitat: Pastures, roadsides and other disturbed ground.

Range: Native to Eurasia, B.C. to Oregon.

SMALL-LEAVED MONTIA

Montia parviflora

Plant: A somewhat succulent perennial 5-30 cm tall.

Flower: 5 white to pink petals 7-15 mm long, usually 3-8 flowers together in a cluster above the leaves.

Leaves: Basal leaves oblanceolate, 1.5-4 cm long, the few stem leaves smaller and narrower.

Habitat: Moist areas in both forests and meadows, and on cliffs.

Range: Alaska to California.

ROSACEAE · ROSE FAMILY

GOATSBEARD

Aruncus sylvester

Plant: An upright, shrub-like perennial that grows to 2.5 m tall in one season, then dies back to the ground.

Flower: Tiny 1 mm white flowers bloom together on pencil-sized stems on upper branches.

Leaves: Pinnately compound with ovate, serrate leaflets with pointed tips.

Habitat: Along roadsides, moist woods and moist forest openings, streambanks.

Range: Alaska to California.

15

BUCKBEAN

Menyanthes trifoliata

Plant: An aquatic to semi-aquatic perennial 10-40 cm tall.

Flower: Petals fused together, corolla with 5-6 white lobes, often pink-tinged, with long white hairs.

Leaves: On long stems and palmately compound, with three elliptical leaflets 4-12 cm long.

Habitat: Lakes, ponds, bogs.

Range: Alaska to California.

ONE-SIDED WINTERGREEN

Pyrola secunda

Plant: A small, spreading perennial 5-15 cm tall.

Flower: 5 white petals each 4-5 mm long, 6-20 flowers, consistently along one side of upper stem.

Leaves: Ovate, 1.5-6 cm long, all along stem, well below flowers.

Habitat: In forest habitats, usually with conifers.

Range: Throughout much of North America.

BEACH CARROT
Glehnia littoralis

Plant: A ground-hugging perennial typically growing in sand at the ocean.

Flower: Tiny white flowers are gathered together in 5-16 ball-like clusters.

Leaves: All basal, pinnately compound, thick, firm, serrate and ground-hugging.

Habitat: Coastal dunes and sandy beaches.

Range: Alaska to California.

SINGLE DELIGHT
Pyrola uniflora

Plant: A diminutive perennial 3-15 cm tall with a single flower.

Flower: White, 1.5-2.5 cm wide at top of nearly leafless stem. Prominent and protruding style/stigma.

Leaves: Basal or nearly so, ovate, 1-2.5 cm long, lightly serrate along the edges.

Habitat: In coniferous forests.

Range: Alaska to Oregon.

17

THIMBLEBERRY
Rubus parviflorus

Plant: An upright, thornless shrub .5-2 m tall, with gray, flaking bark.

Flower: 5 white petals 1.5-2.5 cm long, with numerous stamens, usually several flowers together at stem tips.

Fruit: Red, like a raspberry, edible, sweet to somewhat bitter.

Leaves: Large and maple-like, with 3-5 sharp-pointed lobes and serrate edges, 6-15 cm long and at least as wide.

Habitat: Moist to dry woods and meadows, sea level to subalpine mountains.

Range: Alaska to Oregon.

CREEPING RASPBERRY
Rubus pedatus

Plant: A low, mat-forming, thornless perennial to 10 cm tall.

Flower: The white-petaled flowers are 1-2 cm across and have reflexed sepals, bloom singly on naked stems.

Fruit: Small clusters of red berries, edible, juicy and tasty.

Leaves: Palmately compound, with 5-7 leaflets, leaves 4-10 cm wide, attached at the ground.

Habitat: Moist woods, from sea level to timberline.

Range: Alaska to Oregon.

HIMALAYAN BLACKBERRY

Rubus discolor

Plant: An erect shrub with long, arching canes to 4 m long, and heavy recurved thorns with sharp brambles.

Flower: White to pink, 5-petaled flowers are 2 cm wide, several together at branch tips.

Fruit: Blackberries, very popular for eating.

Leaves: Palmately compound, 5-10 cm long, usually with 5 ovate and serrate leaflets.

Habitat: Roadsides and disturbed ground west of the Cascades at lower elevations.

Range: A noxious but tasty weed from Eurasia, now common from B.C. to California.

TRAILING BLACKBERRY

Rubus ursinus

Plant: A sprawling and trailing perennial with stems to 6 m long, armed with slender, backward-pointing thorns.

Flower: White, male (petals 12-18 mm) and female (petals 8-12 mm) flowers on different plants.

Fruit: Blackberries, edible and delicious.

Leaves: Pinnately compound, with 3 ovate and serrate leaflets, the terminal one 6-10 cm long.

Habitat: Open to dense woods and open disturbed sites.

Range: B.C. to California.

19

FIELD BINDWEED

Convolvulus arvensis

Plant: A trailing and climbing perennial with stems up to 2 m long.

Flower: Corolla vase-shaped, white to pink, 1.5-2.5 cm long, typically two flowers per leaf axil.

Leaves: Usually arrow-shaped, the blade 2-6 cm long, arranged singly along stem.

Habitat: Disturbed ground at lower elevations.

Range: Introduced from Europe, now widely established in North America.

RANUNCULACEAE · BUTTERCUP FAMILY

FALSE BUGBANE

Trautvetteria caroliniensis

Plant: An erect perennial that spreads from rhizomes, 40-80 cm tall.

Flower: Petals lacking, the 4 sepals whitish, 3-5 mm long, stamens many and white.

Leaves: Mostly basal, wider than long, deeply lobed into 3-5 serrate segments.

Habitat: Moist woods and along streams.

Range: B.C. to California.

WHITE MORNING-GLORY
Convolvulus sepium

Plant: A trailing and climbing perennial 2-3 m long.

Flower: Corolla vase-shaped, white to pink, 4-7 cm long, typically 1 flower per leaf axil.

Leaves: Arrow-shaped, 5-12 cm long, arranged singly along stem.

Habitat: Moist soil, especially along river bottoms and coastal marshes.

Range: A native of the eastern U.S., now in moist areas throughout the West.

BEACH MORNING GLORY
Convolvulus soldanella

Plant: A creeping perennial 10-40 cm long, with fleshy leaves.

Flower: Corolla vase-shaped, pink, 3-5 cm long, typically 1 flower per leaf axil.

Leaves: Kidney-shaped, much wider than long, 1.5-4 cm broad, arranged singly along stem.

Habitat: Coastal beaches and sand dunes.

Range: B.C. to California.

21

TWISTED STALK

Streptopus amplexifolius

Plant: An upright, branching perennial 30-80 cm tall.

Flower: Greenish-white, 1 per leaf axil under the leaves, dangling from a twisting stalk.

Leaves: Elliptic and parallel-veined, 5-12 cm long, clasping the stem.

Habitat: Moist places in forests and along streams.

Range: Throughout North America.

DEVIL'S CLUB

Oplopanax horridum

Plant: An erect to sprawling shrub 1-3 m tall, abundantly armed with yellow spines.

Flower: Small (5-6 mm long) white flowers in 1-2 cm wide clusters along upright stem.

Leaves: Large, maple-like, 7-9 lobed, serrate, 10-35 cm wide.

Habitat: Moist woods, along streams at low to middle elevations.

Range: B.C. to Oregon.

LILIACEAE · LILY FAMILY

WHITE FAWN LILY

Erythronium oregonum

Plant: A delicate, 2-leaved perennial 10-30 cm tall.

Flower: 1-3 blooms per plant, the 6 narrow tepals white, 4-5 cm long, drying pinkish.

Leaves: 2 opposite leaves on stem, narrowly elliptic and mottled, 8-20 cm long.

Habitat: Moist lowlands, woods to prairies.

Range: B.C. to Oregon.

LILIACEAE · LILY FAMILY

QUEEN'S CUP, BEAD LILY

Clintonia uniflora

Plant: A delicate perennial, 7-15 cm tall, rhizomatous and forming colonies.

Flower: Usually 1 flower per plant on an erect stem with 6 white tepals.

Fruit: One white or blue berry 6-10 mm long at top of stem.

Leaves: 2 or 3 elliptic leaves opposite each other on the stem, 7-15 cm long.

Habitat: Moist coniferous forests.

Range: Alaska to California.

23

WESTERN TRILLIUM

Trillium ovatum

Plant: An erect perennial plant 10-40 cm tall.

Flower: 1 white blossom in center of plant just above whorl of leaves, the 3 petals white, aging pink, 3-8 cm long.

Leaves: 3 broadly ovate leaves, 5-15 cm long, in a whorl near stem apex.

Habitat: Moist woods and along streams.

Range: B.C. to California.

WESTERN LILY OF THE VALLEY

Maianthemum dilatatum

Plant: A rather delicate perennial from spreading rhizomes (and therefore colonial), 10-40 cm tall.

Flower: 4 white tepals each about 2.5 mm long, with 10-50 flowers along on an upright stem.

Fruit: Each flower produces a red berry, 5-6 mm long.

Leaves: Typically two heart-shaped (cordate) leaves per stem, 5-10 cm long.

Habitat: Moist woods and along streams.

Range: Alaska to California.

OXEYE DAISY

Chrysanthemum leucanthemum

Plant: An upright perennial 20-80 cm tall.

Flower: A composite, composed of white ray flowers (petals) 1-2 cm long and yellow disk flowers in the center.

Leaves: Basal leaves obovate, the blade 2-8 cm and deeply toothed, stem leaves smaller and narrower.

Habitat: Fields, roadsides and other disturbed ground.

Range: A native of Eurasia, now common throughout much of temperate North America.

VANILLA LEAF

Achlys triphylla

Plant: A perennial 20-50 cm tall, plants often numerous from spreading rhizomes, often gives off a vanilla odor when dry.

Flower: Tiny white flowers gathered in an upright spike above the leaves.

Leaves: Palmately compound and basal, held upright on a long (10-30 cm) stalk, 3 large fan-shaped leaflets, blunt-toothed or wavy.

Habitat: Moist forests and along streams.

Range: B.C. to California.

25

WHITE SWEET CLOVER
Melilotus alba

Plant: An erect, branching annual or biennial .5-3 m tall.

Flower: White, small (5 mm), and pea-like, many clustered together along elongate stems.

Leaves: Compound, with 3 leaflets, elliptic and roughly serrate.

Habitat: Disturbed ground, pastures, roadsides.

Range: Native of Eurasia, now throughout temperate North America.

SIBERIAN MINER'S LETTUCE
Montia sibirica

Plant: An annual or short-lived perennial 10-40 cm tall.

Flower: 5 spreading white to pink petals 6-12 mm long, many flowers gathered together on upright stems.

Leaves: Basal, elliptic, on long petioles, also 2 opposite stem-less leaves on stem.

Habitat: In moist, shady places, from low to midelevations.

Range: Alaska to California.

LEGUMINOSAE · PEA FAMILY

WHITE CLOVER

Trifolium repens

Plant: A low-growing, creeping perennial with stems 10-60 cm long.

Flower: White to pink, pea-like, 5-9 mm long, many clustered together in round heads.

Leaves: A "three-leaf clover," each leaf being divided into 3 rounded leaflets.

Habitat: Disturbed ground.

Range: Native of Eurasia, now widespread in North America.

RANUNCULACEAE · BUTTERCUP FAMILY

BANEBERRY

Actaea rubra

Plant: An upright, branching perennial 40-100 cm tall.

Flower: Many tiny (petals 2-4 mm) white flowers gathered in several close clusters above leaves.

Fruit: Red or occasionally white berries.

Leaves: All on stem, 2-3 times compound, the segments ovate and sharply toothed and lobed.

Habitat: Moist woods and along streams.

Range: Throughout much of North America.

Note: The berries, foliage and roots of this species are highly poisonous.

27

DEATH CAMAS

Zigadenus venenosus

Plant: Narrowly erect, grass-like perennial 10-50 cm tall.

Flower: Many small, white flowers clustered at top of an upright stem.

Leaves: Mostly basal, 10-30 cm long and 3-6 mm wide, few and much smaller up the stem.

Habitat: Variable, coastal meadows to sagebrush and forest edge.

Range: B.C. to California.

Note: The underground bulb is deadly poisonous.

REDWOOD SORREL

Oxalis oregana

Plant: A perennial 5-20 cm tall.

Flower: 5 white to pink, dark-veined petals, flowers borne singly on long stems.

Leaves: All basal but with long petioles (stalks), divided into 3 clover-like leaflets.

Habitat: Moist forests.

Range: B.C. to California.

28

CARYOPHYLLACEAE · PINK FAMILY

FIELD CHICKWEED

Cerastium arvense

Plant: A clumped to matted perennial 5-50 cm tall.

Flower: 5 white petals 8-12 mm long and deeply lobed at the tip.

Leaves: Opposite, narrowly lanceolate, 1-3 cm long.

Habitat: Dry to moist open ground, from meadows to cliffs.

Range: Throughout North America.

APIACEAE · PARSLEY FAMILY

QUEEN ANNE'S LACE

Daucus carota

Plant: A single-stemmed biennial 20-120 cm tall.

Flower: Hundreds of tiny yellow-white flowers gathered in multiple balled clusters atop a long stem.

Leaves: 5-15 cm long and 2-7 cm wide, finely divided like a carrot leaf.

Habitat: Disturbed ground in moist meadows, fields, and along roadsides.

Range: Native of Eurasia, the wild ancestor of the domestic carrot, Alaska to Oregon.

29

FRINGECUP

Tellima grandiflora

Plant: An erect, hairy-stemmed perennial 20-80 cm tall.

Flower: 5 fringed, greenish-white petals (aging red) 4-8 mm, 10-35 flowers along upright stalk.

Leaves: Mostly basal, ovate, lobed and serrate, 3-8 mm long and wide, with hairy stems.

Habitat: Moist woods and along streams, from low to midelevations.

Range: Alaska to California.

NARROW-LEAF SUNDEW

Drosera anglica

Plant: A low-growing, insect-eating plant 5-25 cm tall.

Flower: Small, white, at the top of a naked stem.

Leaves: Blades long and narrow (usually twice as long as wide), the margins covered in reddish glandular hairs with sticky fluid to trap insects.

Habitat: Swamps, bogs, saturated meadows, at low to midelevations.

Range: Alaska to California.

COW PARSNIP
Heracleum lanatum

Plant: A stout, single-stemmed perennial 1-3 m tall.

Flower: Many tiny white flowers gathered in multiple crowded clusters, the overall inflorescence 10-20 cm wide.

Leaves: Huge leaves divided into three large, lobed and toothed leaflets, each 10-40 cm long and wide.

Habitat: Open, wet ground and along streams, from the coast to midmountains.

Range: Throughout North America.

FOAMFLOWER
Tiarella trifoliata

Plant: An erect perennial 10-60 cm tall.

Flower: The 5 white petals are so narrow as to be linear, 2-3 mm long, 5-30 flowers on upright stem.

Leaves: 1.5-7 cm long, compound, divided into three toothed leaflets.

Habitat: In conifer forests from low to subalpine elevations.

Range: Alaska to Oregon.

31

FOOL'S ONION

Brodiaea hyacinthina

Plant: A narrow, upright perennial 20-70 cm tall.

Flower: Corolla white to blue, 10-16 mm long, the lobes twice as long as the fused portion, 5-20 flowers together at top of bare stem.

Leaves: 1 or 2 grass-like leaves, 10-40 cm long and 3-10 mm wide.

Habitat: Meadows and rocky flats, lowlands to midmontane.

Range: B.C. to California.

SAXIFRAGACEAE · SAXIFRAGE FAMILY

EARLY SAXIFRAGE

Saxifraga integrifolia

Plant: A tufted perennial with bare flower stalk 10-40 cm tall.

Flower: 5 white to yellow petals 2-4 mm long, 5-25 flowers clustered at top of stem.

Leaves: In a basal clump, lance-shaped, 2-6 cm long.

Habitat: Wet to dry meadows and grassy slopes.

Range: B.C. to California.

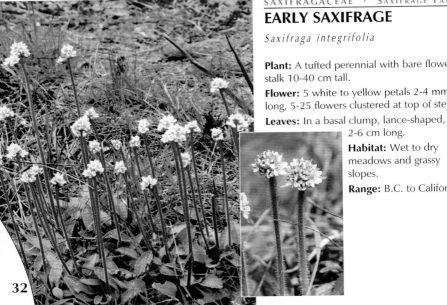

32

AMERICAN SEAROCKET

Cakile edentula

Plant: A sprawling annual with stems 10-50 cm long.

Flower: 4 white to purplish petals 6-8 mm long, blooming in clusters at stem tips.

Leaves: Oblong and oblanceolate, 2-7 cm long, wavy-margined to lobed.

Habitat: Sandy beaches.

Range: Native of the east coast, now B.C. to California.

HAIRY MANZANITA

Arctostaphylos columbiana

Plant: An erect to spreading evergreen shrub with reddish bark, 1-3 m tall.

Flower: Clusters of white to pink, goblet-shaped flowers 6-7 mm long.

Leaves: Ovate to elliptic, 2-5 cm long and 1-2.5 cm wide, pointed at the tip.

Habitat: Sunny, open places along the coast.

Range: B.C. to California.

BLADDER CAMPION

Silene vulgaris

Plant: A branching perennial 10-60 cm tall.

Flower: 5 deeply lobed white petals, the visible, unfused portion 4-6 mm long.

Leaves: Very narrowly elliptic and opposite one another on stem, 3-8 cm long.

Habitat: Disturbed ground at low elevations.

Range: Introduced from Europe, now throughout North America.

WHITE CAMPION

Lychnis alba

Plant: Biennial or perennial with several stems, 20-80 cm tall.

Flower: 5 deeply lobed white petals, the visible, unfused portion 7-10 mm long.

Leaves: Narrowly elliptic and opposite one another on the stem, 5-10 cm long.

Habitat: Disturbed ground at low elevations.

Range: A native of Europe, now widespread in North America.

THYME-LEAVED SPEEDWELL

Veronica serpyllifolia

Plant: A spreading perennial from creeping rhizomes, stems 10-30 cm long.

Flower: Corolla 4-8 mm wide, slightly asymmetrical, in leaf axils, fruit heart-shaped.

Leaves: Broadly elliptic, 1-2.5 cm long, opposite one another along stem.

Habitat: Moist meadows and moist, disturbed ground.

Range: Widespread in North America.

STICKY FALSE ASPHODEL

Tofieldia glutinosa

Plant: A rather delicate, grass-like, perennial 10-50 cm tall, the upright stem sticky-glandular.

Flower: Numerous small (tepals 3-5 mm) white flowers clustered together at stem apex.

Leaves: Few and linear, 5-15 cm long, 3-8 mm wide.

Habitat: Moist open areas, meadows, bogs and along streams.

Range: Throughout much of northern North America.

35

BUTTER AND EGGS, COMMON TOADFLAX

Linaria vulgaris

Plant: An erect and often branching perennial 20-80 cm tall.

Flower: Snapdragon-like, 2-3.5 cm long, bright yellow with an orange throat.

Leaves: Numerous up the stems, linear, 2-10 cm wide.

Habitat: Disturbed ground, pastures, meadows, fields, roadsides.

Range: A native of Eurasia, now widespread in temperate North America.

PINEAPPLE WEED

Matricaria matricarioides

Plant: An annual 5-40 cm tall, pineapple-scented when the flowers are crushed.

Flower: A yellow composite, made of a 5-10 mm wide head of disk flowers only (no ray flowers).

Leaves: Pinnately compound, finely divided and fern-like, 1-5 cm long.

Habitat: Disturbed ground, roadsides.

Range: Alaska to Oregon.

SMALL MONKEY-FLOWER
Mimulus alsinoides

Plant: An upright annual 3-25 cm tall, somewhat viscid (slippery) to the touch.

Flower: Corolla yellow, with a red spot on lower lip, flowers 2 per leaf axil.

Leaves: Elliptic to ovate with a pointed tip, opposite on stem.

Habitat: Moist, shady places, mossy ledges.

Range: B.C. to California.

YELLOW MONKEY-FLOWER
Mimulus guttatus

Plant: Can be a small, 2 cm high annual or perennial to 1 m tall.

Flower: Yellow corolla 1-4 cm, lower lip red dotted, upper tooth of calyx (the fused sepals) longer than the others.

Leaves: Ovate with point at tip, serrate, opposite on stem.

Habitat: Wet ground, seepages, springs, wet meadows, along streams.

Range: Alaska to Oregon.

37

BIRDSFOOT TREFOIL

Lotus corniculatus

Plant: A low, spreading perennial to 5-20 cm tall.

Flower: 3-15 yellow pea-like flowers, sometimes red-tinged, gathered in a rounded cluster atop a bare stem.

Leaves: Pinnately compound, mostly with 5 leaflets, the terminal one 5-15 mm long.

Habitat: Moist soil at lower elevations.

Range: A native of Europe, now B.C. to Oregon.

COMPOSITAE · COMPOSITE FAMILY

GOLD STAR

Crocidium multicaule

Plant: A delicate, upright annual 5-25 cm tall with woolly hair in the leaf axils.

Flower: A composite, with 5-12 yellow ray flowers (petals) 5-10 mm long, the center disk flowers yellow as well.

Leaves: A basal tuft of leaves, oblanceolate, 1-2.5 mm long, stems leaves small and narrow.

Habitat: Dry, open places at lower elevations.

Range: Vancouver Island to Oregon.

SCOTCH BROOM

Cytisus scoparius

Plant: A large, unarmed, branching shrub to
3 m tall.

Flower: Yellow, pea-like, 1.5-2.5 cm long,
1 per leaf axil.

Leaves: Divided into 3 leaflets below, undi-
vided above, .5-2 cm long.

Habitat: Open and disturbed areas from the
coast to low mountains.

Range: A native of Europe, now common
from B.C. to California, an attractive but very
aggressive invasive species.

GORSE

Ulex europaeus

Plant: A stiff shrub 1-3 m tall, fiercely armed
with sharp spines.

Flower: Yellow, pea-like, 15-20
mm long, borne on spiny side
branches.

Leaves: Nearly leafless, those
present rigid and spiny.

Habitat: Disturbed ground at lower
elevations.

Range: A native of Europe, now
B.C. to California.

39

OREGON GRAPE
Berberis nervosa

Plant: A spreading shrub with evergreen leaves, 10-60 cm tall.

Flower: Bright yellow, with 6 bilobed petals, flowers 10-40 on narrow spike.

Fruit: Blue, rounded, 8-11 mm long.

Leaves: Pinnately compound, with 9-19 leaflets holly-like, ovate-elliptical, with 3 main veins and spiny teeth.

Habitat: In open to closed-canopy forests, low to moderate elevations.

Range: B.C. to California.

CAPRIFOLIACEAE · HONEYSUCKLE FAMILY

BLACK TWINBERRY
Lonicera involucrata

Plant: A widely branching shrub to 4 m tall.

Flower: Tubular yellow flowers arranged in pairs in leaf axils, surrounded by reddish bracts.

Fruit: 1 black, round fruit per flower, 1 cm wide, 2 per leaf axil.

Leaves: Elliptic, 5-14 cm long with pointed tip, opposite one another on stem.

Habitat: In moist to wet soil, lowlands to upper mountains.

Range: Alaska to Oregon.

RANUNCULACEAE · BUTTERCUP FAMILY

CREEPING BUTTERCUP

Ranunculus repens

Plant: A low, spreading, hairy perennial 5-20 cm tall.

Flower: Usually 5 yellow petals (sometimes more) 7-17 mm long.

Leaves: Compound, 3-7 cm, with 3 leaflets, each deeply lobed and toothed.

Habitat: Moist, open areas, especially on disturbed ground.

Range: A native of Europe, Alaska to Oregon.

RANUNCULACEAE · BUTTERCUP FAMILY

WESTERN BUTTERCUP

Ranunculus occidentalis

Plant: An upright, hairy perennial 15-40 cm tall.

Flower: 5 yellow petals 9-12 mm long, flowers few to many at top of stem.

Leaves: Variable, with 3 ovate lobes lower on plant, and 3 narrow, point lobes higher up.

Habitat: Moist, open areas, coast to midmountains.

Range: Alaska to California.

YELLOW SAND VERBENA
Abronia latifolia

Plant: A glandular-hairy, prostrate and trailing perennial with stems to 1 m long.

Flower: Yellow-green tubular flowers with yellow lobes 5-7 mm across, in clusters at top of short stems.

Leaves: Thick and fleshy, widely ovate, 1.5-4 cm long.

Habitat: Coastal beaches.

Range: Vancouver Island to California.

FOOTSTEPS OF SPRING
Sanicula arctopoides

Plant: A taprooted perennial with either prostrate or ascending stems 5-30 cm long.

Flower: Tiny yellow flowers are gathered in 1 cm wide clusters, and these are surrounded by a ring of long bracts.

Leaves: Mostly basal, succulent, deeply 3-cleft and somewhat triangular in shape, 2.5-6 cm long and up to 9 cm wide.

Habitat: Coastal bluffs.

Range: Vancouver Island to California.

SIERRA SANICLE
Sanicula graveolens

Plant: A single-stemmed, taprooted perennial 5-50 cm tall.

Flower: Tiny yellow flowers gathered together into 1 cm wide rounded clusters at stem apex.

Leaves: Stems long compared to blade, leaves divided in 3 leaflets and these deeply lobed.

Habitat: Dry, open forests and rocky slopes from low to moderate elevations.

Range: B.C. to California.

PACIFIC SANICLE
Sanicula crassicaulis

Plant: A single-stemmed, taprooted perennial 25-120 cm tall.

Flower: Tiny yellow flowers gathered in several 1 cm wide clusters at top of largely bare stem.

Leaves: Generally wider than long and deeply 3-lobed, these again lobed and serrate.

Habitat: Moist and dry woods.

Range: B.C. to Oregon.

43

SMOOTH HAWKSBEARD
Crepis capillaris

Plant: An erect annual or biennial 10-80 cm tall.

Flower: A composite, composed entirely of yellow ray flowers about 1 cm long, 5-25 flower heads at top of stem.

Leaves: Oblanceolate, 3-30 cm long and 5-40 mm wide, the upper with little 'ears' (auricles) where they meet the stem.

Habitat: Meadows, pastures, lawns and other disturbed ground.

Range: A native of Europe, now from B.C. to California.

ROSACEAE · ROSE FAMILY

LARGE-LEAVED AVENS
Geum macrophyllum

Plant: An upright perennial 20-70 cm tall.

Flower: Petals yellow, 4-6 mm long, the sepals reflexed, usually several flowers together on upright stems.

Leaves: Pinnately compound with 7-21 serrate leaflets, the one at the tip much the largest, the entire leaf 10-30 cm long.

Habitat: Moist woods and meadows, along streams, from sea level to subalpine.

Range: Alaska to Oregon.

44

BLADDERWORT

Utricularia vulgaris

Plant: A submerged, free-floating aquatic that sends flower stalks above water, this is a carnivorous plant that traps tiny aquatic animals in small bladders on the leaves.

Flower: 1-20 yellow, bilateral flowers 1-2 cm long, borne on stem emerging from water.

Leaves: Numerous, 1-5 cm long, finely divided into pitchfork-like segments.

Habitat: In ponds and lakes, low to midelevations.

Range: Alaska to Oregon.

YELLOW POND LILY

Nuphar polysepalum

Plant: An aquatic perennial with broad, floating leaves.

Flower: Large yellow flowers with petals (in this case actually sepals) 3-6 cm long.

Leaves: Big, 10-40 cm long, cordate (heart-shaped), mostly floating.

Habitat: Ponds and lakes.

Range: Alaska to California.

ST. JOHN'S-WORT

Hypericum perforatum

Plant: An erect, branching perennial 10-60 cm tall.

Flower: 5 yellow petals 8-14 mm long, with numerous stamens.

Leaves: Lanceolate, 1-3 cm long, opposite on the stem, with small 'perforations' in the leaf blade.

Habitat: Disturbed ground, pastures, fields, roadsides, streambeds.

Range: Native of Europe, now B.C. to Oregon.

PRICKLY SOWTHISTLE

Sonchus asper

Plant: A tall weedy species, with a hollow stem and milky juice, 10-100 cm tall.

Flower: Yellow, ray flowers only, several heads in flat clusters.

Leaves: Alternate, clasping stem, upper leaves elliptical, toothed or lobed.

Habitat: Roadsides, disturbed sites, fields from low to midelevations.

Range: A native of Europe, in our range now B.C. to Oregon.

STREAM VIOLET
Viola glabella

Plant: Our most common yellow violet, an upright perennial 5-30 cm tall.

Flower: Yellow, with purple lines on lower petals.

Leaves: Cordate (heart-shaped), 3-10 cm long, basal ones on long petioles (stems).

Habitat: Moist woods and along streams from low to subalpine elevations.

Range: Alaska to California.

LANCE-LEAVED STONECROP

Sedum lanceolatum

Plant: A succulent perennial 5-20 cm tall.

Flower: 5 yellow petals with pointed tips, in clusters of 10-50 at stem tips.

Leaves: Linear but fleshy and rounded, 5-20 mm long.

Habitat: Open, often rocky ground, sea level to subalpine.

Range: Alaska to California.

BROAD-LEAVED STONECROP

Sedum spathulifolium

Plant: A succulent perennial 5-20 cm tall.

Flower: 5 yellow petals with pointed tips, in clusters of 10-50 at stem tips.

Leaves: Oblong to spoon-shaped, fleshy, 10-20 mm long.

Habitat: Coastal cliffs and gravelly soil at low to midelevations.

Range: B.C. to Oregon.

GUMWEED

Grindelia integrifolia

Plant: An upright perennial 15-80 cm tall.

Flower: Composite, the yellow rays about 1 cm long, the bracts below the rays sticky.

Leaves: Oblanceolate, the basal ones 5-40 cm long and 1-4 cm wide, smaller up the stem.

Habitat: At edge of salt marshes, along rocky shores, and open meadows.

Range: Alaska to Oregon.

CRUCIFERAE · MUSTARD FAMILY

FIELD MUSTARD

Brassica campestris

Plant: An upright, branching annual 10-80 cm tall.

Flower: 4 yellow petals, flowers crowded at stem tips, fruits long and narrow.

Leaves: Lower ones compound, with the end leaflet far the largest, upper ones oblong and clasping the stem.

Habitat: Disturbed ground, especially pastures and farm fields.

Range: A native of Eurasia, now throughout much of North America.

49

DANDELION
Taraxacum officinale

Plant: A tufted perennial with milky juice, the flower stalk 5-50 cm tall.

Flower: Yellow composite heads composed of many ray flowers.

Leaves: Basal, oblanceolate, deeply toothed (dandelion means 'tooth of the lion'), 6-40 cm long.

Habitat: Disturbed ground, lawns at low to midelevations.

Range: Native of Eurasia, now throughout North America.

HAIRY CATS-EAR
Hypochaeris radicata

Plant: A dandelion-like perennial with basal leaves and flower stalk 10-60 cm tall.

Flower: A composite yellow head made up entirely of ray flowers (no disk flowers), one to several per stem.

Leaves: Basal, oblanceolate, deeply toothed, 2.5-15 cm long.

Habitat: Meadows, pastures, lawns, roadsides.

Range: A native of Europe, now throughout much of temperate North America.

SPRING GOLD
Lomatium utriculatum

Plant: An upright perennial 10-60 cm tall.

Flower: Tiny yellow flowers gathered together into several 1 cm wide, rounded heads at apex of plant.

Leaves: Leaves finely divided like those of a carrot plant, most of them on the upright stem.

Habitat: Dry, open rocky slopes and grassy bluffs and meadows.

Range: B.C. to Oregon.

GOLDENROD
Solidago canadensis

Plant: Narrow, upright perennial, spreading colonially from rhizomes, 20-150 cm tall.

Flower: Tiny composite heads crowded together in a pyramidal to spike-like cluster at top of plant.

Leaves: Almost entirely on the stem (no basal cluster), narrowly elliptic, serrate to entire, 5-15 cm long.

Habitat: Moist soil in meadows, streambanks, open places.

Range: Throughout most of North America.

51

STICKY CINQUEFOIL
Potentilla glandulosa

Plant: An upright perennial 10-50 cm tall, often with sticky glandular hairs on the stems and leaves.

Flower: Petals pale to deep yellow, 5-10 mm long, in clusters of 5-20 on upright stems.

Leaves: Pinnately compound, with 5-9 ovate and strongly serrate leaflets.

Habitat: Wet to dry meadows and forest openings.

Range: B.C. to Oregon.

GRACEFUL CINQUEFOIL
Potentilla gracilis

Plant: An upright, usually rather hairy perennial 30-60 cm tall.

Flower: Petals yellow, obovate, often dented at the tip, about 1 cm long, flowers in flat-topped clusters.

Leaves: Palmately compound, the 5-9 leaflets narrowly elliptic, deeply serrate and 3-8 cm long.

Habitat: In a variety of open habitats, moist to dry.

Range: Alaska to Oregon.

SULFUR CINQUEFOIL

Potentilla recta

Plant: An upright perennial 20-60 cm tall, short hairy and sometimes glandular.

Flower: Petals yellow, 6-12 mm long, obovate and indented at the tip, usually 3-10 flowers together in flat-topped, upright clusters.

Leaves: Palmately compound, with 3-5 narrowly elliptic and deeply serrate leaflets.

Habitat: Disturbed, open ground.

Range: Originally from Eurasia, now widely established in North America.

COMMON MULLEIN

Verbascum thapus

Plant: An erect biennial to 2 m tall, with large, fuzzy leaves forming a rosette the first year.

Flower: 4 yellow petals, flowers 1-2 cm wide, many crowded together on stiff, upright spike.

Leaves: Elliptic and very hairy, lower ones 10 -40 cm, upper ones clasping the stem.

Habitat: Disturbed ground at lower elevations.

Range: Native of Eurasia, now throughout temperate North America.

SKUNK CABBAGE

Lysichiton americanum

Plant: A perennial 30-150 cm tall with a skunky odor.

Flower: Yellow, tiny, many crowded together on upright spike surrounded by cupped, leafy bract.

Leaves: Large, 30-100 cm long, ovate to oblong.

Habitat: Wet, often shaded ground.

Range: Alaska to Oregon.

WORMSEED MUSTARD

Erysimum cheiranthoides

Plant: An upright annual 30-80 cm tall with few or no branches.

Flower: 4 yellow petals 3.5-5 mm long, flowers clustered in elongate head at top of stem, fruits narrow, erect.

Leaves: Very narrowly elliptic, 3-8 cm long and .5-1.8 cm wide.

Habitat: Moist, disturbed sites at low elevations.

Range: Widespread in North America.

YELLOW RATTLE

Rhinanthus minor

Plant: Narrow, erect annual 15-60 cm tall.

Flower: Yellow, the bilateral corolla 9-14 mm long, largely hidden by the calyx (the fused sepals).

Leaves: Lanceolate to ovate, serrate, long, opposite one another up stem.

Habitat: Meadows, grassy hillsides, beaches.

Range: Alaska to Oregon.

RANUNCULACEAE · BUTTERCUP FAMILY

LITTLE BUTTERCUP

Ranunculus uncinatus

Plant: An upright perennial with 1 to few stems 20-60 cm tall.

Flower: 5 yellow petals 2-3 mm long, with, 1-10 flowers at branch ends, the fruits with hooked tips.

Leaves: Basal leaves triangular in outline and deeply 3-lobed and serrate, upper 3-lobed but much narrower.

Habitat: Moist woodlands, thickets and meadows.

Range: Alaska to Oregon.

COMPOSITAE · COMPOSITE FAMILY

TANSY
Tanacetum vulgare

Plant: A stout, aromatic, upright perennial 40-150 cm tall, rhizomatous and colonial.

Flower: Small, round yellow composite heads with disk flowers only, numerous heads are gathered together in a flat-topped cluster.

Leaves: Pinnately compound with 7-17 leaflets, the leaflets narrow and deeply toothed.

Habitat: Disturbed ground in fields and meadows, and along streambanks and roadsides.

Range: A native of Eurasia, now throughout North America.

LEGUMINOSAE · PEA FAMILY

BLACK MEDIC
Medicago lupulina

Plant: A finely hairy, trailing annual with stems 10-40 cm long.

Flower: Tiny 2-3 mm pea-like flowers, 10-40 clustered together in short spikes on a bare stem.

Leaves: Compound, divided into 3 oval clover-like leaflets.

Habitat: Disturbed ground in meadows, pastures, roadsides.

Range: Introduced from Europe, now throughout North America.

GNOME PLANT

Hemitomes congestum

Plant: A small, pink to brown perennial of coniferous forests, 3-20 cm tall.

Flower: 4 pink-drying-brown petals are fused into a tubular corolla, 12-20 mm long, 5-20 flowers are congested at the stem tip.

Leaves: Small leaves are reduced to scale-like bracts pressed against the stem.

Habitat: In deep humus in coniferous forests.

Range: B.C. to California

Note: Gnome plant is a saphrophye, rather than photosynthesizing to produce its food supply, it breaks down dead organic material.

ARISTOLOCHIACEAE · BIRTHWORT FAMILY

WILD GINGER

Asarum caudatum

Plant: A low, creeping, matted perennial 5-30 cm high.

Flower: Purple-brown, with 3 long-tapered 'petals' 3-8 cm long, flowers solitary, hidden at ground level by leaves.

Leaves: Cordate (heart-shaped), 4-10 cm long and 5-15 cm wide, opposite each other on stem.

Habitat: Moist, shady woods.

Range: B.C. to Oregon.

CAPRIFOLIACEAE · HONEYSUCKLE FAMILY

ORANGE HONEYSUCKLE

Lonicera ciliosa

Plant: A vine that climbs to 6 m.

Flower: Tubular corolla orange, 2.5-4 cm long, in dense clusters of 5-25 at stem ends.

Leaves: Broadly elliptic, 4-10 cm long, opposite one another on stem, uppermost pair fused together.

Habitat: Forests and shrub thickets, from low to midelevations.

Range: B.C. to California.

PRIMULACEAE · PRIMROSE FAMILY

SCARLET PIMPERNEL

Anagallis arvensis

Plant: A prostrate to ascending annual with stems 10-40 cm long.

Flower: Corolla lobes salmon-pink, the flower 5-8 mm wide, on bare stalks from leaf axils.

Leaves: Ovate, 5-15 mm long, opposite one another up stem.

Habitat: Disturbed, open ground at low elevations.

Range: Native of Eurasia, now Vancouver Island to California.

PAPAVERACEAE · POPPY FAMILY

CALIFORNIA POPPY

Eschscholzia californica

Plant: A taprooted perennial 10-50 cm tall.

Flower: Deep yellow to orange, 4 obovate petals 6-20 cm long, flowers close at night.

Leaves: Finely divided, somewhat resembling carrot leaves but gray-green in color.

Habitat: Open meadows and hills at low elevations.

Range: Native to California and Oregon, now in B.C. and Washington as well.

COMPOSITAE · COMPOSITE FAMILY

ORANGE HAWKWEED

Hieracium aurantiacum

Plant: A rhizomatous perennial with a basal tuft of leaves and an upright flower stalk 20-60 cm tall.

Flower: Several composite heads crowded together at top of nearly leafless stem, each composed of orange ray flowers.

Leaves: Basal and narrowly oblong, 5-20 cm, with bristly hairs on both surfaces.

Habitat: Disturbed ground with adequate moisture.

Range: A native of Europe, now present from B.C. to California.

RED FLOWERING CURRANT
Ribes sanguineum

Plant: Upright shrub 1-3 m tall.

Flower: Tubular, rose-red flowers with spreading lobes 1 cm across, 10-20 blooming together, blooms in early spring.

Leaves: Triangular, deeply 3-lobed and serrate, 2.5-6 cm wide.

Habitat: Open, dry woods, roadsides, logged areas from low to midelevations.

Range: B.C. to California.

RANUNCULACEAE · BUTTERCUP FAMILY

RED COLUMBINE
Aquilegia formosa

Plant: An upright perennial to 20-80 cm tall.

Flower: Red, sepals petal-like, 1.5-2.5 cm long, the shorter petals forming a spur, flower with many protruding stamens.

Leaves: Doubly compound, with 3 leaflets again divided in 3s, the final segments lobed.

Habitat: Moist areas in both meadows and open forests.

Range: Throughout western North America.

STRIPED CORAL ROOT
Corallorhiza striata

Plant: Narrow, erect perennial 15-40 cm tall, stems red-purple.

Flower: 7-30 small pink orchids on upright stem, the lower petal (lip) with dark stripes.

Leaves: Green leaves absent, the plant being saprophytic (gathers nutrients from decaying organic matter).

Habitat: In coniferous and deciduous forests from low to midelevations.

Range: B.C. to California.

SPOTTED CORAL ROOT
Corallorhiza maculata

Plant: A narrow, erect perennial 20-40 cm tall, stems red-purple.

Flower: 10-30 small pink orchids on upright stem, the lower petal (lip) red-spotted.

Leaves: Green leaves absent, the plant saprophytic (gathers nutrients from decaying organic matter).

Habitat: In coniferous and deciduous forests.

Range: Throughout temperate North America.

FIREWEED
Epilobium angustifolium

Plant: Erect perennial 1-3 m tall, spreading widely from rhizomes.

Flower: 4 clawed (narrowed at base), rose-colored petals, the flowers 1-2 cm across, numerous, blooming continuously up erect stem.

Leaves: Very narrowly elliptic, 10-15 cm long, alternate up the stem.

Habitat: In disturbed sites, including burns, roadsides, riverbanks.

Range: Throughout North America.

SELF HEAL
Prunella vulgaris

Plant: Erect to prostrate, clumped to matted perennial 5-40 cm tall.

Flower: Corolla violet, 1-2 cm long, bilaterally symmetrical, hooded, flowers crowded in dense heads at stem tips.

Leaves: Lanceolate to narrowly elliptic, 2-9 cm long, opposite one another on stem.

Habitat: Moist, open ground, lowlands to midelevations.

Range: Alaska to Oregon.

CRUCIFERAE · MUSTARD FAMILY
SWEET ROCKET
Hesperis matronalis

Plant: An erect perennial with 1 to several stems, 40-120 cm tall.

Flower: 4 petals, rose to white, flowers 1-2 cm wide, fragrant, clustered toward top of plant.

Leaves: Lanceolate to elliptic, serrate, 5-20 cm long.

Habitat: On disturbed, open ground in the lowlands.

Range: An escaped garden flower native of Europe, now B.C. to California.

ORCHIDACEAE · ORCHID FAMILY
CALYPSO ORCHID
Calypso bulbosa

Plant: A delicate perennial 5-20 cm tall.

Flower: Red-pink sepals and petals narrow and upright above, white-to-purple lower lip, flowers usually solitary, fragrant.

Leaves: One ovate-elliptic basal leaf, 3-6 cm long.

Habitat: Moist to dry forests with abundant organic matter in soil.

Range: Alaska to California.

COMMON STORK'S-BILL

Erodium cicutarium

Plant: Small, taprooted annual 4-30 cm tall.

Flower: 5 pink petals, flowers 10-15 mm wide, resulting fruit enlongating greatly to resemble the bill of a stork.

Leaves: Mostly basal, pinnately compound with the leaflets deeply incised.

Habitat: Disturbed, open ground at low elevations.

Range: Native of Eurasia, now widespread in western North America.

SALAL

Gaultheria shallon

Plant: Sprawling shrub 1-3 m tall.

Flower: 5-15 pink, goblet-shaped flowers, each 7-10 mm long, along stems near branch tips.

Fruit: Purplish or reddish stalks, edible.

Leaves: Ovate-elliptic, 5-9 cm long and distinctly serrate.

Habitat: Open ground and coniferous forests, from the coast to lower mountains.

Range: Alaska to California.

PACIFIC RHODODENDRON
Rhododendron macrophyllum

Plant: Upright evergreen shrub 1-6 m tall.

Flower: Pink, 5-lobed corolla (petals fused) 2.5-4 cm long, many flowers together in terminal clusters.

Leaves: Oblong elliptic and leathery, 8-20 cm long.

Habitat: Coniferous forests along the coast.

Range: B.C. to California.

BALDHIP ROSE
Rosa gymnocarpa

Plant: Slender, rather straggling shrub 30-120 cm tall with slender thorns.

Flower: Petals pink to rose, flowers mostly borne singly on short stems arising from leaf axils.

Fruit: The name 'baldhip' comes from the fact that the fruit or rosehip has no sepals left attached at its tip.

Leaves: Pinnately compound, the 5-9 leaflets elliptical and strongly serrate, each 1-4 cm long.

Habitat: Moist to dry woods and forest edges.

Range: B.C. to California.

FIELD MINT

Mentha arvensis

Plant: Fragrant, upright perennial 1-60 cm tall, spreading from creeping rhizomes.

Flower: Tiny (2.5-3 mm), pink to white, gathered in clusters in leaf axils.

Leaves: Elliptic and serrate, 2-8 cm long, opposite one another on stem.

Habitat: Moist to wet open places, especially along streams and lakeshores.

Range: Alaska to Oregon.

MARSH VIOLET

Viola palustris

Plant: Low perennial 4-30 cm tall, spreading from rhizomes and stolons.

Flower: Petals lilac to white, with purple lines on the lower 3, flowers 10-13 mm long, on naked stems.

Leaves: Cordate (heart-shaped), on long stems (petioles), 2.5-3.5 cm wide, with wavy margins.

Habitat: In moist meadows, wetland edges, along streams.

Range: B.C. to California.

SALMONBERRY
Rubus spectabilis

Plant: A rhizomatous and colonial perennial 1-4 m tall, the stems arching, shredding bark, thorny to unarmed.

Flower: Petals reddish-pink and showy, obovate-elliptic, 12-20 mm long, blooming singly or several together.

Fruit: Yellow to red/magenta, large and edible.

Leaves: Compound, with 3 ovate, strongly serrate and pointed leaflets.

Habitat: Moist woods and streambanks, lowlands to midmontane.

Range: Alaska to California.

PRINCE'S PINE, PIPSISSEWA
Chimaphila umbellata

Plant: Small, evergreen shrub 10-35 cm tall.

Flower: 5 pink, spreading petals, each 5-7 mm long, 5-15 flowers together at top of bare stem.

Leaves: Narrowly elliptic and sharply serrate, 3-7 cm long and .5-2.5 cm wide.

Habitat: Coniferous forests at low to midelevations.

Range: Throughout much of North America.

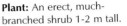
HARDHACK
Spiraea douglasii

Plant: An erect, much-branched shrub 1-2 m tall.

Flower: Tiny flowers have pink petals 1-2 mm long, hundreds bloom together in upright clusters.

Leaves: Oblong-elliptic, 3-9 cm long, serrate at the tip only.

Habitat: Wet meadows, stream banks, bogs, low to high elevations.

Range: Alaska to California.

POLYGONACEAE · BUCKWHEAT FAMILY

WATER SMARTWEED
Polygonum amphibium

Plant: An aquatic to amphibious (wet shorelines) perennial, stems freely rooting.

Flower: Pink, quite small at 4-5 mm, but 50-150 clustered together in tight heads on stems above water.

Leaves: Elliptic, usually floating, 5-15 cm long.

Habitat: Shallow ponds and lakes.

Range: Widespread in North America.

FOXGLOVE
Digitalis purpurea

Plant: Erect, unbranched perennial usually 1-2 m tall.

Flower: Pink-purple corolla 4-6 cm long, many flowers bloom along erect stem.

Leaves: Ovate and serrate, the lower ones 10-40 cm long, getting smaller up the stem.

Habitat: Disturbed, open ground, especially roadsides, forest edges.

Range: Native to Europe, now B.C. to California.

BLEEDING HEART
Dicentra formosa

Plant: Erect, rhizomatous, spreading perennial 15-45 cm tall.

Flower: Corolla pink, flattened, heart-shaped at the base and short lobes at the tip, 2-20 flowers blooming together at top of bare stem.

Leaves: 10-40 cm long, 3 times compound, the ultimate segments quite narrow.

Habitat: Moist woods, along streams.

Range: B.C. to California.

HEDGE-NETTLE

Stachys cooleyae

Plant: A hairy, spreading perennial 5-120 cm tall, usually with a single stem.

Flower: Corolla red-purple, bilaterally symmetrical, with a long lower lip 8-14 mm long, blooming in whorls on upper stem.

Leaves: Ovate, 6-15 cm long, serrate, opposite one another on stem.

Habitat: Wet ground, swamps.

Range: B.C. to Oregon.

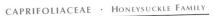

SNOWBERRY

Symphoricarpos albus

Plant: A branching shrub to 1.5 m high.

Flower: Small pink tubular flowers are 4-6 mm long, with 1 to several growing at branch tips.

Fruit: The white, round fruits give the plant its common name.

Leaves: Elliptic to oblong, 2-6 cm long, opposite one another on the stem, sometimes toothed or lobed.

Habitat: Open forests, forest edges, shrublands, and riparian areas.

Range: Alaska to California.

BEARBERRY, KINNIKINNICK
Arctostaphylos uva-ursi

Plant: A low, spreading, often matted evergreen shrub with reddish bark, to 10 cm high.

Flower: Small, pinkish, goblet-shaped long, growing several together at stem tips.

Fruit: Bright red berries 7-10 mm across, edible, but mealy and tasteless.

Leaves: Obovate, leathery and evergreen, 1.5-3 cm long.

Habitat: In dry, open areas from low elevations to alpine zone.

Range: Throughout North America.

SEA BLUSH
Plectritis congesta

Plant: Slender, upright perennial 10-60 cm tall.

Flower: Corolla 2-8 mm long, pink or white, bilateral with protruding lower lip and a spur protruding backwards.

Leaves: Relatively few, opposite one another on stem, obovate, 1-6 cm long.

Habitat: Vernally moist meadows and open slopes.

Range: Vancouver Island to California.

71

ROSE CAMPION

Lychnis coronaria

Plant: Few-branched, gray-hairy perennial 30-80 cm tall.

Flower: Petals deep red to purple, spreading, flower 2-3 cm wide, several blooming at top of upright stem.

Leaves: Basal leaves oblanceolate, 5-10 cm long, stem leaves smaller, elliptical, opposite one another.

Habitat: Disturbed ground at lower elevations.

Range: Native of Europe, now B.C. to Oregon.

SCENTED POND LILY

Nymphaea odorata

Plant: Rooted aquatic perennial of shallow water, with nearly round floating leaves.

Flower: White, tinged with pink, fragrant, with 20-30 petals 4-8 cm long, closing in afternoon.

Leaves: Heart-shaped, nearly round, 10-25 cm across.

Habitat: Ponds, shallow lakes, irrigation ditches.

Range: Native to eastern U.S., now widely introduced B.C. to California.

BULL THISTLE
Cirsium vulgare

Plant: Upright biennial .5-1.5m tall with spiny winged membranes on the stem.

Flower: Several purple composite heads at apex of plant, each 2-6 cm wide, composed only of disk flowers.

Leaves: Oblanceolate, 5-20 cm long, deeply incised into narrow segments with spiny tips.

Habitat: Disturbed ground, pastures, grazed meadows, logged areas, roadsides.

Range: Native of Eurasia, now throughout much of North America.

CANADA THISTLE
Cirsium arvense

Plant: Rhizomatous, stickery, upright perennial 30-150 cm tall that forms extensive stands.

Flower: 5-30 purple composite heads, each about 1 cm wide, clumped together near apex of plant.

Leaves: Narrowly elliptical, the lower leaf edges wavy, the upper deeply toothed, all are spiny.

Habitat: Moist, disturbed ground.

Range: A native of Eurasia, now throughout much of North America.

73

DOVEFOOT GERANIUM

Geranium molle

Plant: Spreading, hairy annual 10-40 cm tall.

Flower: 5 pink petals, tips notched, flowers typically in pairs, fruit elongate like a crane's bill.

Leaves: Almost round in outline, but deeply 5-9 lobed, 6-14 cm wide.

Habitat: Moist, disturbed ground.

Range: A native of Europe, now widespread in North America.

HERB ROBERT

Geranium robertianum

Plant: Taprooted, branching annual 10-50 cm tall.

Flower: 5 pink to purple petals, often with areas of white.

Leaves: Triangular in outline, very deeply lobed, the main segments again deeply dissected.

Habitat: On disturbed ground, but also colonizes moist, open forests and dry, rocky outcrops.

Range: A native of Eurasia, now a troublesome weed B.C. to California.

APOCYNACEAE · DOGBANE FAMILY

SPREADING DOGBANE

Apocynum androsaemifolium

Plant: A branching, upright perennial 20-50 cm tall, with milky juice.

Flower: Corolla fused, 5-9 mm long, with 5 erect lobes, flowers in clusters near stem ends.

Leaves: Elliptic to ovate, 2.5-7 cm long, opposite on the stem and frequently drooping.

Habitat: Dry soil in meadows, hills, forest edges.

Range: Widespread in North America.

FUMARIACEAE · FUMITORY FAMILY

SCOULER'S CORYDALIS

Corydalis scouleri

Plant: An erect, thinly branching perennial 40-100 cm tall.

Flower: Corolla pink with a backwards-pointing spur, flowers on upright spike.

Leaves: Usually only 3 leaves, on the stem, several times compound, the ultimate leaflets 2-6 cm long.

Habitat: Moist soil in partial to deep shade.

Range: B.C. to Oregon.

PINK FAWN LILY
Erythronium revolutum

Plant: Erect perennial 10-30 cm tall with two mottled green leaves.

Flower: Usually 1 or 2 per plant, tepals pink, 3.5-4 cm long, tips curved backwards.

Leaves: 2, opposite each other on stem, mottled green, elliptic, 12-18 cm long.

Habitat: Moist, open woods, forest edges, river banks.

Range: B.C. to California.

EVERGREEN HUCKLEBERRY
Vaccinium ovatum

Plant: Erect but bushy evergreen shrub 1-4 m tall.

Flower: Clusters of 3-10 small pink, bell-shaped flowers at stem tips.

Fruit: Small, purple to black, edible, somewhat sweet.

Leaves: Narrowly ovate with pointed tips, 2-5 cm long, neatly arranged along stem.

Habitat: In and near coniferous forests and on beaches, coast to low mountains.

Range: B.C. to California.

PLUMBAGINACEAE · PLUMBAGO FAMILY

THRIFT, SEA-PINK

Armeria maritima

Plant: A grasslike perennial 10-50 cm tall.

Flower: 5 pink to lavender petals, flowers many in compact heads at top of leafless stem.

Leaves: Many narrow, grasslike leaves in basal clump, each 5-10 cm long.

Habitat: Beaches and coastal bluffs.

Range: Alaska to California.

COMPOSITAE · COMPOSITE FAMILY

PINK PUSSYTOES

Antennaria rosea

Plant: A low, mat-forming, spreading, gray and hairy perennial 5-40 cm tall.

Flower: Several small, white to red, rayless (no petals) heads gathered together at the top of a stem, resembling the paw of a pussycat.

Leaves: Most leaves basal, oblanceolate, 1-3 cm long and 2-7 mm wide, gray-hairy.

Habitat: Dry, open places at low and midelevations.

Range: Alaska to California.

SPRINGBANK CLOVER
Trifolium wormskjoldii

Plant: A taprooted sprawling perennial with stems 10-80 cm long.

Flower: Pea-like in heads of 2-60 flowers subtended by ragged bracts.

Leaves: Compound leaves with 3 elliptic leaflets, 1-3 cm long.

Habitat: From coastal dunes to meadows and stream banks.

Range: B.C. to California.

PERENNIAL PEA
Lathyrus latifolius

Plant: Sprawling, rhizomatous perennial 40-150 cm tall.

Flower: Pea-like, red-pink or occasionally white, 1.5-2 cm long, 5-15 on upright stems.

Leaves: Compound, but with only two elliptic leaflets 7-14 cm long, opposite each other, with tendrils at leaf tip.

Habitat: Disturbed ground, also on clay banks near ocean.

Range: Native to Europe, now throughout temperate North America.

VARI-LEAVED COLLOMIA

Collomia heterophylla

Plant: Branched, leafy, 5-40 cm tall, somewhat slimy/hairy on upper portions.

Flower: Pink or lavender, five short lobes spreading from tube.

Leaves: Alternate, toothed, with long spreading hairs.

Habitat: Streambanks, forest openings, meadows, roadsides, low elevations.

Range: B.C. to Oregon.

RED CLOVER

Trifolium pratense

Plant: Soft-hairy, erect to spreading, taprooted perennial 20-60 cm tall.

Flower: Red, pea-like flowers 13-20 mm long, 50-200 clustered in tight, round heads.

Leaves: The quintessential 3-leaf clover, although in fact it's 3 leaflets.

Habitat: Fields, meadows, disturbed ground, roadsides.

Range: A native of Europe, now widespread in North America.

MUSK MALLOW
Malva moschata

Plant: Upright perennial 20-50 cm tall.

Flower: 5 pink to white, spreading petals, flowers 4-5 cm across, 1-10 blooming at top of stem.

Leaves: Variable, lower cordate, upper cleft to the base in 5 lobes and these again dissected.

Habitat: Disturbed ground, roadsides.

Range: Native to Europe, now B.C. to Oregon.

CLUSTERED CANCER ROOT
Orobanche grayana

Plant: An upright perennial 5-12 cm tall, lacking green leaves, parasitic on composite family.

Flower: Corolla purple, 2-3 cm long, with 5 lobes, 2-30 flowers crowded together.

Leaves: Lacks green leaves.

Habitat: Meadows and open slopes.

Range: B.C. to California.

NODDING ONION

Allium cernuum

Plant: Grass-like plant with 2-6 leaves and a nodding flower head 10-40 cm tall.

Flower: Tepals pink to white, ovate, 4-6 mm long, 8-30 flowers together in a nodding head.

Leaves: Long and narrow, shorter than the flower head.

Habitat: Moist, often shady sites, lowlands to midmontane.

Range: Widespread in North America.

BEACH PEA

Lathyrus japonicus

Plant: Spreading, rhizomatous perennial to 1.5 m, often trailing or climbing on other plants.

Flower: Reddish-purple to blue, pea-like, 2-8 flowers together on upright stem.

Leaves: Compound, with 6-12 elliptic leaflets 2-5 cm long and tendrils at leaf tip.

Habitat: Sandy areas, beaches amongst driftwood.

Range: Alaska to California.

PURPLE LOOSESTRIFE

Lythrum salicaria

Plant: Erect, rhizomatous, spreading perennial to 2 m, known to take over wetlands and choke out native plants.

Flower: 5 red-purple petals, flowers crowded together in elongated spikes at top of stem.

Leaves: Lanceolate, 3-10 cm long, mostly (but not all) opposite each other on stem.

Habitat: Wetlands, stream banks, lakeshores.

Range: A native of Europe, now a beautiful but noxious weed throughout temperate North America.

PACIFIC WATERLEAF

Hydrophyllum tenuipes

Plant: Erect perennial 20-80 cm tall.

Flower: 5 greenish white to purple petals, clustered in heads of 15-50 flowers.

Leaves: Few and large, 5-15 cm long and wide, with 5-7 deep lobes or leaflets, and these sharply toothed.

Habitat: Moist forests at low to moderate elevations.

Range: B.C. to California.

LEAFY PEAVINE

Lathyrus polyphyllus

Plant: Sprawling, spreading, rhizomatous perennial 30-80 cm tall.

Flower: Red to purple, pea-like, 5-13 flowers along one side of stem.

Leaves: Pinnately compound, with 10-16 elliptical leaflets 2.5-6 cm long and tendrils at leaf tip.

Habitat: Open fields to partial shade in lowlands and foothills.

Range: B.C. to California.

TUFTED VETCH

Vicia cracca

Plant: Sprawling, climbing perennial .5-1 m tall.

Flower: Pea-like, violet-purple, with 20-70 flowers together along one side of upright stem.

Leaves: Pinnately compound, 6-12 cm long, with 12-18 linear, opposite leaflets and tendrils at leaf tips.

Habitat: Disturbed areas, fields, meadows, roadsides.

Range: Native of Eurasia, now widespread in North America.

SALSIFY, OYSTER PLANT
Tragopogon porrifolius

Plant: Stiffly upright, milky-juiced biennial 30-80 cm tall.

Flower: Large composite head 3-7 cm wide, composed entirely of purple ray flowers.

Leaves: Long and narrow, 10-30 cm long and 5-30 mm wide.

Habitat: Disturbed ground with somewhat moist soil.

Range: Formerly a cultivated plant from Europe, now through much of temperate North America.

PURPLE NIGHTSHADE, BITTERSWEET NIGHTSHADE
Solanum dulcamara

Plant: Spreading perennial with stems 1-3 m long, often sprawling over other plants.

Flower: Corolla violet-blue, with lobes (petals) 5-9 cm long and bent backwards, 10-25 flowers in a loose cluster.

Fruit: Berries mature to a bright red, resembling miniature tomatoes to which they are related.

Leaves: Ovate with point tips, 2.5-8 cm, sometimes with 2 basal lobes.

Habitat: Thickets, clearings, deciduous woods, usually where moist to wet.

Range: Native of Eurasia, now throughout temperate North America.

SATIN FLOWER

Sisyrinchium douglasii

Plant: Grass-like, narrowly erect perennial 10-30 cm tall.

Flower: 6 tepals reddish purple, oblanceolate, 15-20 mm long.

Leaves: Basal leaves reduced, 1-2 cm long, the 4-10 grass-like stem leaves 5-15 cm long.

Habitat: Variable, open meadows to sage and pine, but usually where moist at least in spring.

Range: B.C. to California.

BLACK LILY, RICE LILY

Fritillaria camschatcensis

Plant: Narrow, upright perennial 20-50 cm tall with several dark flowers and narrow leaves in whorls on stem.

Flower: 6 green-brown to purple tepals 2-3 cm long, flowers bell-shaped, 1-7 blooming at top of stem.

Leaves: 1-3 whorls of 5-9 narrow leaves on the single, upright stem, each 4-10 cm long.

Habitat: Moist areas, from lowlands to midmontane.

Range: Alaska to Washington.

85

BROAD-LEAVED SHOOTING STAR

Dodecatheon hendersonii

Plant: Narrow perennial with all-basal leaves and upright flower stalk 10-30 cm.

Flower: Corolla magenta, with petals swept backwards, 2-15 flowers.

Leaves: Basal, ovate to broadly elliptic, 3-8 cm long.

Habitat: Meadows, rocky bluffs, stream banks, often where wet in spring.

Range: B.C. to California.

FEW-FLOWERED SHOOTING STAR

Dodecatheon pulchellum

Plant: Narrow perennial with all-basal leaves and upright flower stalk 10-40 cm.

Flower: Corolla pink to lavender, long, with petals swept backwards, 1-20 flowers.

Leaves: All basal, narrowly elliptic, 2-15 cm long.

Habitat: Wet areas, from coastal prairies to mountain meadows.

Range: Throughout much of North America.

CHOCOLATE LILY

Fritillaria lanceolata

Plant: Narrow, upright perennial 15-80 cm tall with dark, pendant flowers.

Flower: 6 purplish tepals 2-3 cm long, mottled with yellow/green, 1-5 flowers per plant.

Leaves: On stem only, narrowly lanceolate, 5-15 cm long, in 1-2 whorls on stem plus several scattered above.

Habitat: Variable, open grassy areas to deciduous and conifer forests.

Range: B.C. to California.

ALFALFA

Medicago sativa

Plant: Taprooted, generally erect, branching perennial 30-80 cm tall.

Flower: Blue-purple, pea-like, 1 cm long, 20-100 flowers blooming together in upright heads.

Leaves: Compound, with three elliptic, serrate leaflets 2-4 cm long.

Habitat: Disturbed ground, fields, roadsides, riverbanks.

Range: Native of Eurasia, now escaped from cultivation throughout temperate North America.

MARSH CINQUEFOIL

Potentilla palustris

Plant: Perennial growing in or near shallow water, reddish stems often floating.

Flower: 5 red to purple petals which are quickly decidous (fall off), leaving spreading purple sepals behind.

Leaves: Pinnately compound, the 5-7 leaflets oblong-elliptic and strongly serrate, each 3-8 cm long.

Habitat: Wet meadows, pond and lake margins, bogs, low to high elevations.

Range: Alaska to California.

 OROBANCHACEAE · BROOMRAPE FAMILY

NAKED BROOMRAPE

Orobanche uniflora

Plant: Small erect plant 2-10 cm tall, parasitic on stonecrop, saxifrage and composites.

Flower: Corolla purple to yellow, 15-35 mm long, the 5 lobes finely fringed, flowers solitary on stems.

Leaves: Lacking green leaves.

Habitat: Variable, moist to dry, open to light woods.

Range: Widespread in North America.

COAST PENSTEMON
Penstemon serrulatus

Plant: Erect, several-stemmed perennial 20-70 cm tall.

Flower: Corolla blue to purple, 10-30 flowers in a rather tight cluster at top of stem.

Leaves: All on stem, ovate, pointed and sharply serrate, 3-8 cm long, opposite each other on stem.

Habitat: Meadows, along streams, open woods, where moist or wet.

Range: B.C. to Oregon.

MANY-LEAVED LUPINE
Lupinus polyphyllus

Plant: Tall and striking perennial lupine, 40-100 cm tall.

Flower: Blue and pea-like, 10-15 mm long, many flowers together in upright spikes 15-40 cm long.

Leaves: Palmately compound, hairless at least on top, with 9-15 narrowly elliptic leaflets, each 4-10 cm long.

Habitat: Moist open forests, meadows, and along streams.

Range: B.C. to California.

CHICORY
Cichorium intybus

Plant: A taprooted, upright perennial with milky juice, 30-120 cm tall.

Flower: Composite heads with blue ray flowers 1-2 cm long, 1 to 3 heads together along the stem.

Leaves: Mostly basal, oblanceolate, deeply toothed, 8-25 cm long.

Habitat: Dry to moist disturbed ground.

Range: A native of Eurasia, now throughout temperate North America.

RANUNCULACEAE · BUTTERCUP FAMILY

POISON LARKSPUR
Delphinium trollifolium

Plant: Stiffly upright perennial, with 1 to several stems 50-120 cm tall.

Flower: Flaring sepals, petal-like, small inner petal nearly white, flowers blooming progressively at top of plant.

Leaves: Lower ones nearly circular but deeply 3-lobed, these lobes also deeply incised, upper leaves narrower.

Habitat: Moist woods and along streams.

Range: Washington to California.

GREAT CAMAS

Camassia leichtlinii

Plant: Narrow, grasslike perennial 20-50 cm tall.

Flower: 6 spreading, blue-violet tepals, each 2.5-3.5 cm long, with many flowers along the upright stem.

Leaves: 2-8 narrow, grasslike leaves low on stem, 20-60 cm long.

Habitat: Meadows and hills where moist in spring.

Range: B.C. to California.

CAMAS

Camassia quamash

Plant: Narrow, grass-like perennial 20-70 cm tall.

Flower: 6 blue to violet tepals 1.5-3.5 cm long, the lowest curving outward, away from stem, flowers many along upright stem.

Leaves: 2-8 narrow, grasslike leaves low on stem, 20-60 cm long.

Habitat: Meadows and forest edges, where moist in spring.

Range: B.C. to California.

GERANIACEAE · GERANIUM FAMILY

NORTHERN GERANIUM
Geranium erianthum

Plant: Upright, branching perennial 10-50 cm tall.

Flower: 5 blue-purple petals with darker purple penciling.

Leaves: Basal leaves in a rosette, heart-shaped but deeply lobed into 7 segments.

Habitat: Moist meadows and forest edges.

Range: Alaska to B.C.

RANUNCULACEAE · BUTTERCUP FAMILY

MENZIE'S LARKSPUR
Delphinium menziesii

Plant: Upright perennial 10-60 cm tall with hairy stem.

Flower: Petal-like sepals deep blue, long, few-to-many flowers in terminal cluster.

Leaves: Nearly round in outline but deeply 2-3 times dissected, 3-7 cm across.

Habitat: Grassy meadows and rocky bluffs.

Range: B.C. to California.

SMALL-FLOWERED LUPINE

Lupinus polycarpus

Plant: Annual, erect stems, 10-45 cm tall, striking brownish-hairy plant.

Flower: Deep blue and white, pea-like, in small clusters.

Leaves: Palmately compound, 5-8 leaflets 4 cm long.

Habitat: Open, gravelly and sandy sites at low elevations.

Range: B.C. to Oregon.

SMALL BLUE-EYED MARY

Collinsia parviflora

Plant: Diminutive, branching annual, typically less than 10 cm tall.

Flower: Corolla small, 4-8 mm, bilateral, blue with white upper lip, growing from leaf axils.

Leaves: Narrowly elliptic, 1-5 cm long, opposite or whorled on stem.

Habitat: Dry hillsides, rocky slopes, forest edges, with adequate moisture in spring.

Range: Aiaska to California.

Index of Common and Scientific Names